Python Machine Learning

A Crash Course for Beginners to Understand Machine learning, Artificial Intelligence, Neural Networks, and Deep Learning with Scikit-Learn, TensorFlow, and Keras.

by

Josh Hugh Learning

Josh Hugh Learning

this book, without the consent of the author or publisher.

Disclaimer Notice:

Please note the information contained within this document is for educational and entertainment purposes only. All effort has been executed to present accurate, up to date, and reliable, complete information. No warranties of any kind are declared or implied. Readers acknowledge that the author is not engaging in the rendering of legal, financial, medical or professional advice. The content within this book has been derived from various sources. Please consult a licensed professional before attempting any techniques outlined in this book.

By reading this document, the reader agrees that under no circumstances is the author responsible for any losses, direct or indirect, which are incurred as a result of the use of information contained within this document, including, but not limited to, — errors, omissions, or inaccuracies.

Table of Contents

Introduction

Congratulations on purchasing Python Machine Learning, and thank you for doing so.

The following chapters will discuss a lot of the different parts that we need to know when it is time to start working with the Python language and getting it to work for some of your own machine learning needs. There are many companies that want to work with machine learning in order to help them learn more about their company, their competition, their industry, and their customers. When we collect the right data and combine it with the right machine learning algorithms, we will be able to make this work for our needs

Sometimes, getting started with machine learning is hard, and knowing how to get your own program set up and ready to go will be important. The hardest part is figuring out the algorithms that we are going to spend some time working on along the way. There are really quite a few machine learning algorithms that you are able to work with, and picking the right one often will depend on the different processes that you want to do, the questions that you want the data to answer for you, and even the kind of data that you are trying to work with.

We are going to look at some of the basics that come with the process of machine learning and how to pick out the kind of data that we are able to work with as well. Then we will spend the rest of this guidebook looking at some of the different algorithms that we want to handle in this kind of language, with the help of Python. These will ensure that we are able to take over make sure that our data is handled and that we are actually able to see results with the work that we need to do.

There are many types of algorithms that we are able to explore. Some of the options that we are going to explore in this guidebook will include regressions, linear classification, non-linear, and more. In each of these categories, we are going to spend our time looking at how we can get started with this process, and the types of algorithms that fit into each one, and more. When you are done with this guidebook, you will know what you need about some of the most common machine learning algorithms and how to use them for your own data analysis.

There is so much that we are able to do with the Python language, and learning how to use it to pick out the right machine learning can be important. When you are ready to get started with Python machine learning, make sure to check out this guidebook to help you get started.

There are plenty of books on this subject on the market, thanks again for choosing this one! Every effort was made to ensure it is full of as much useful information as possible, and please enjoy it!

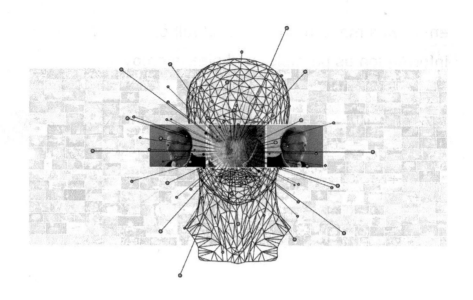

Chapter 1: The Basics of Machine Learning

The first topic that we need to spend some time working on in this guidebook is information on machine learning and what we are able to do with it. This is a huge word in the technology and business world, but many people are not certain about what this all means, and how they are able to work with machine learning to reach some of their own goals along the way.

To start with, we need to take a look at what machine learning is all about and why it is gaining so much popularity in our world today. Machine learning is basically an application of artificial intelligence that is going to provide our systems with the ability to automatically learn and improve from experience, without being programmed on everything that they should be doing. Machine learning focuses on the creation and improvement computer programs that can access data and then use this data to learn.

It all starts with observations, or even data, such as instructions, direct experiences, and examples, in order to look for patterns in data and make better decisions in the future based on the example that we provide. The primary aim is to allow these computers a way to learn without any assistance or intervention from humans automatically, and then you can see that the computer will be able to adjust their actions accordingly to work with this as well.

There are a lot of applications that go with machine learning, and we are going to spend time in this guidebook looking at a lot of the different algorithms and more that you are able to do with machine learning. When you get all of this working together, you will see some amazing results and really see the true potential that comes with machine learning.

There are a lot of different things that you are able to use in machine learning. Any time that you aren't sure how the end result is going to turn up, or you aren't sure what the input of the other person could be, you will find that machine learning can help you get through some of these problems. If you want the computer to be able to go through a long list of options and find patterns or find the right result, then machine learning is going to work the best for you.

Some of the other things that machine learning can help out with include:

1. Voice recognition
2. Facial recognition

3. Search engines. The machine learning program is going to start learning from the answers that the individual provides, or the queries, and will start to give better answers near the top as time goes on.

4. Recommendations after shopping

5. Going through large amounts of data about finances and customers and making accurate predictions about what the company should do to increase profits and happy customers along the way.

These are just a few of the examples of when you would want to start utilizing a program that needs to be able to act on its own. Many of the traditional programs that you are going to learn how to use as a beginner are going to be much simpler than this. They will tell the computer exactly what it should do in a given situation. This works great for a lot of programs, but for things like artificial intelligence, it is not going to be enough.

In addition, you will find that this machine learning is going to be a really good thing to use when it comes to handling data analysis, which is what some of the algorithms that we will discuss in this guidebook are used for in most cases. There are many algorithms that happen with this, but knowing how to use them and how they fit in with not only machine learning but also data science is going to be important.

Data analysis is going to be really important when it comes to your business and how competitive you can be in the future. You will find that with the right algorithms, and the information that we are going to go through in this guidebook with those algorithms, you will be able to handle some of the different business problems you have, complete your data analysis, and finally gain a good understanding of what all that big data you have been collecting is all about.

The Benefits of Machine Learning

There are actually quite a few benefits that we are going to see when it comes to working with machine learning on a regular basis. This is most likely one of the major reasons why so many companies want to jump on board and see what this is all about. Depending on the kinds of questions that you are looking to answer about your business and more, you will be able to find an application of machine learning in no time.

Machine learning is going to simplify some of the steps that come with product marketing and can assist when you want to make accurate forecasts of sales. Machine learning is going to be able to do this in more than one manner. For example, you will be able to get through a massive amount of data from as many sources as you want. There is likely to be a lot of information in there to help you modify and review all of your marketing strategies until you get the most effective one. You will also find that machine learning can help with rapid analysis, prediction and processing, and it is good at interpreting the past behaviors of your customers.

All of these come together to help you quite a bit, you will be able to use this unlimited amount of information in order to learn more about the customer, figure out what they are looking for in your business, and learn the best way to reach them in the marketing that you do. Considering marketing is an important part of the success of any business, you can easily see why so many companies want to be able to use this for themselves as well.

Machine learning can also help to facilitate accurate diagnoses and predictions in the medical field. This kind of learning is going to help doctors to identify their high-risk patients, make good diagnoses, and give the best medicines that are possible in each case. These are going to be based, for the most part, on available sets of data on patient records that remain anonymous, as well as the symptoms that these patients were experiencing at the time. This can help doctors and other medical professionals become more efficient at the jobs they are doing for us.

When it is time to really work on data entry, but the work is going to take too long to accomplish manually, machine learning is able to step in and help make this happen easier. Data duplication and inaccuracy are going to be big issues for companies who would like to automate the process of data entry. Machine learning can help work with taking those data entry tasks and getting the work done in no time.

Machine learning is also going to have a big impact on the finance sector. Some of the most common benefits of machine learning when it comes to the financial world will include loan underwriting, algorithmic trading, and fraud detection. In addition, this kind of learning is going to help us with continual data assessments to detect and then analyze any of the anomalies that happen in the financial world, which is going to really help to improve the amount of precision that we can find in our models and rules financially.

We will also see that machine learning is able to help with detecting spam. This was actually one of the earliest problems that machine learning was able to come in and help with. Spam filters are able to make up new rules, using neural networks, in order to eliminate spam mail and keep your inbox as clean as possible. The neural network is able to learn how to recognize phishing messages as well as other junk mail when it evaluates the rules that are found across an ever-growing network of computers.

The manufacturing industry is even able to benefit from some of the things that we see with machine learning. Manufacturing firms need to have corrective and preventative maintenance practices in place. However, these are going to be inefficient and costly in many cases. This is where machine learning can step in to help, and it is going to be a great tool in creating a highly efficient predictive maintenance plan that keeps the business up and running and doing well. In fact, when the company follows these plans, it is going to minimize the chances of failures that are not expected to happen, which will reduce unnecessary preventive maintenance activities.

Machine learning is also going to help with better customer segmentation and accurate lifetime value prediction. These are going to be some of the biggest challenges that marketers are going to face on a daily basis. Marketing and sales units are going to have an enormous amount of data sourced from many channels, but accurate predictions are only going to be found when we look at machine learning.

Some of the best marketers out there right now know that they should use machine learning to eliminate some of the guesswork that comes with their marketing efforts. For example, when they use the data representing the patterns of behavior for their users during a trial period, they are going to be able to help their company make predictions on how likely it is to get conversions to a paid trial and figure out if this paid trial is worth their time or not.

And finally, we are able to look at how machine learning is going to be the right option for recommending products and more to customers. This is one of the best ways for a company to cross-sell and up sell to their customers and can be really useful for customers as well. If you have ever gone onto a website and had something like "customers like you bought these products" or something similar, then you have seen machine learning at work in this way.

The models of machine learning are going to analyze the purchase history that they see with the customer, and based on that, they are able to identify the products that the company has that the customer may be interested in. The algorithm is a good one to help us find the hidden patterns among the items and then will group similar products into clusters. This is going to be a good example of unsupervised learning, which we are going to talk about in a moment.

This kind of model is helpful to businesses because it ensures they are able to provide the best product recommendations back to their customers, which is a great way to motivate customers to make another purchase. In this manner, unsupervised machine learning is going to help us to make a really strong recommendation system for the company and can increase the amount they are going to see in profits along the way.

As we can see, there are a lot of benefits that come with working in machine learning, and companies across all industries out there are going to be able to see some of the benefits. Some of the tasks that come with this is making sure that you collect the right kind of data, and that you take your time to pick out a good algorithm that can actually sort through your data and will help you to really hear the predictions and more that you need.

Supervised Machine Learning

Now there are going to be three types of machine learning that we are able to work with when it comes to the algorithm types. We are going to spend some time looking at each one and how it is meant to work overall. Let us look that the supervised form of machine learning. These can apply what has been learned prior and then putting that towards new data, with the help of examples that are labeled in order to predict whether an event is likely to happen in the future or not.

Beginning from the analysis on a known set of data, the algorithm that you choose here is going to be able to produce for us a function to make predictions about the values we are given. The system, when it is working well, is going to be able to provide targets for any new input after you do enough training on it. The learning algorithm is going to compare the output that it gives with the intended and correct output, then it is able to find out any of the errors that are there modify the models in the right manner along the way.

Along with the same kind of idea, but combining some of the work that we will talk about with unsupervised learning later on, includes semi-supervised machine learning algorithms. It is going to work with labeled and unlabeled data to help with the training. In most cases, we are going to see just a small amount of data that is labeled as being used, and then a large amount of data that is unlabeled that is being used. This is because working with labeled data can be expensive, even when it is efficient, and being able to work with this kind of data is going to be hard to handle, and you will need to add in the unlabeled data to get things done.

The systems that are going to work with this kind of algorithm are going to be higher in the amount of accuracy that they will see with their results. In many cases, this kind of learning is going to be chosen any time that the labeled data that we are working with requires skills and relevant resources in order to either train or learn from it. Otherwise, you will find that acquiring the unlabeled resources and data that you need won't require additional work to get it all done.

Unsupervised Machine Learning

Now that we have had a chance to take a look at what the supervised machine learning algorithms are able to do, it is time to take a look at what we are able to do with unsupervised machine learning algorithms. These are going to be the ones that we use any time that the information we have is used to train the algorithm, and it is not going to be labeled or classified. This means that the algorithm, and the system or machine it is on, will need to do the learning on their own, without examples and labeled data to help it make more sense.

Unsupervised learning studies show a system is able to infer a function to describe one of the hidden structures from the unlabeled data. The system doesn't figure out the right output with this one, it is going to explore the data and then draw inferences from the sets of data.

With this one, we are going to use a lot of data that doesn't have a label on it or any information as to the right answer, and then we are able to send it right through the algorithm and let the system learn along the way. This takes more time, and you may end up with some more runs of training and testing before you are done, but it can be one of the best ways to get some strong systems in place to help with your machine learning.

Reinforcement Machine Learning

This is going to be the method of learning that is going to interact with the environment around it by producing actions, and then discovering the rewards or the errors as it goes on. You can compare this one to the idea of trial and error along the way. The trial and error are going to add to the search and delayed reward and are going to be some of the most relevant characteristics of this kind of learning.

When we work with reinforcement machine learning, we are going to find that it allows the software agents and the machine to automatically, on their own, determine the ideal behavior that they should take to maximize the performance that we are seeing. This is something that we are going to call the reinforcement signal.

When we are looking at reinforcement machine learning, there are going to be a lot of similarities to how the computer learns compared to how a human can learn along the way. This method is set up to help us really be able to work with trial and error, and the computer will be able to use this idea to figure out the right course of action to help them be successful. There is so much that we are able to do when it comes to machine learning, and figuring out these different parts, and how to make them work is a challenge that many data scientists are going to have to deal with on a regular basis. When you are ready to explore more about machine learning, and some of the cool things that you as a programmer can do with this language, make sure to read on through below and see all of the different choices in algorithms and more that are available.

Chapter 2: Learning the Data sets of Python

When it comes to working with machine learning and the Python language, there is nothing better than working with data. The more data that you are able to gather and clean, the easier it is to work with some of the algorithms that come with this process. You will find that Python is going to provide us with many algorithms, but we first need to be able to organize the data and get it set up to go through the algorithms for training and testing, in order to see the results that we would like.

With this in mind, we need to take some time to explore the different types of data that we are able to use. We have to look at some of the differences that come up with unstructured and structured data when to use each one, and how we can use these types of data in order to help us train and test some of our Python machine learning algorithms.

Structured Data Sets

The first type of data that we need to spend time working with is structured data. Traditionally we would just have this kind of data in the past, which was harder to get but was easy to work with. Companies would look for some of the structured data that they need, and then make some of the business decisions and more that they need to move forward.

This kind of data is going to be any data that has been organized well and is then going to fit into a formatted repository for us to use. Usually, this is going to be data that is stored in a database so that the elements can be used for more effective processing and analysis.

We may be able to find this kind of data when we are going through other databases to help with the information, or when we get the results of a survey. This one is much easier to work with because it is already organized, and it is going to fit into the algorithm that you want to work with without you have to worry about missing values, duplicates, outliers, or anything else like this. It is also a much more expensive method of working with data, which can make it harder to work with overall as well.

This is why many companies have to make a balancing act over how much-structured data and how much-unstructured data they want to work with. The structured data can make the work easier and will ensure that the algorithm is going to work better, but it is harder to collect, there is less of it, and it is more expensive. The unstructured data is sometimes hard to work with and takes time to clean and organize, but there are endless amounts of it, it can still be used to handle your machine learning algorithms, and it is a lot less expensive to gather up and use.

Unstructured Data Sets

The second type of data that we need to take a look at is the unstructured data. This is basically going to represent any of the data that doesn't provide us with a recognizable structure to it. It is going to be raw and unorganized, and there may not be any rhyme or reason to what you are seeing. Unstructured data is often going to be called loosely structured data in some cases, where the sources of data may have some kind of structure, but not all of the data in that set will end up following the same structure, so you will still have some work to handle to make them work for your needs.

For those businesses that are going to center around the customer, the data that is found in this kind of form can be examined and there is so much that we are able to get out of it, such as using it to enhance the relationship marketing and the customer relationship management that happens as well. The development of unstructured data, as time goes on, is likely to keep growing because more and more businesses are looking to gather this information, and it can be gathered and created in no time at all.

Unstructured data is going to refer to any data that is able to follow a form that is less ordered than items like a database, table, spreadsheets, and other ordered sets of data. In fact, the term data set is going to be a good way to look at this because it is going to be associated with data that is neat and doesn't have any extra content. We are basically working with a lot of data that is not necessarily organized and can be hard to work with without some help organizing.

There are a ton of instances where we are going to see this kind of data. We may see it in documents, social media posts, medical records, books, collaboration software, instant messages, presentations, and Word documents, to name a few. We are able to work with some non-textual unstructured data, and we will see that this can include video files JPEG images and even some MP3 audio files as well.

Most of the data that you are going to work with over time will rely on the idea of unstructured data. There is so much of this kind of data out there to work with, and it is often easier to find and less expensive compared to some of the structured data that we talked about above. Being prepared to handle some of this unstructured data and make sure that it is prepared and ready to go with some of your machine learning algorithms.

How to Manage the Missing Data

We also need to spend some time working with the missing data that comes in. When we are gathering all of that data from all of those different sources, it is likely that at least some of that data is going to come in missing. Whether this is just one part of the data, or there are a lot of values that are missing for entry, we need to know how we can manage these missing data points.

If we tried to push some of these missing data points through the chosen algorithm, it would not end up going all that well. The algorithm may or may not be able to handle some of the issues with the missing data and even if the algorithm is able to handle the missing values, there could be issues with it skewing the results. This is why it is important to choose which method you would like to use when it is time to manage that missing data.

The method you choose will depend on the type and amount of missing data. If you just have a few points that are missing, then it is probably fine to erase those points and not worry about them at all. This can be the easiest method to work with because you will be able to get them gone in no time. However, for the most part, it is important to keep all of the data that you have, and filling them in is a better way to manage the data.

There are a few ways that you are able to fill in the missing data. Usually, going with the average or the mean of the rest of the data, is going to be a good way to start. This ensures that you are still able to use the data that is missing, while not losing out on some of the important parts that you need with that entry as well. Find the standard that you want to use, and then fill in those missing parts so that the data can work better with the algorithm that we are using.

In addition to the missing data, we need to spend some time learning how to manage the outliers and duplicate content. Both of these, if they are not taken care of, is going to skew the results that you get. It is important to figure out the best way to handle both of these before you move on.

To start, we have the outliers. If you have big outliers that are random but really high or really low compared to the rest of the values, you will find that it is going to mess with your results, and those results are not going to be as accurate as you would like. If this is what happens with your data, then it is probably best to just delete the outlier. It is just something that is not that important, and removing it will ensure that you are able to handle the data in an accurate manner.

Now, there are some situations where the outliers are going to be important, as well. If you are looking at some of the outliers, and it looks like there are a number of outliers that are going to fit into one cluster or group, then this may be a sign that we need to move on to looking at these and using the outliers. If you can see that a significant number of outliers are in this group, rather than just one or two random outliers, then this could be a good sign that there is a new option to work with for reaching customers, marketing, the new product you want to release and more. It never hurts to take a look at these outliers, but for many situations, you will want to delete these.

In addition, we need to focus on the duplicates. Many times we will want to go through and delete the duplicates so that the answers don't end up causing any issues with the results that we have. If you have ten of the same person, with all of the same information for them in your set of data, it is going to skew your results.

If this happens a few times, the issue is going to get even worse overall. For the most part, we want to go through and delete these enough so that we just end up with no duplicates or at least a minimal amount of them.

Splitting Your Data

One thing that we will need to work on when it comes to our data is figuring out how to split it up. There is some work that we have to do in order to handle some of the data that we need before we can go through and add them to the algorithms that we want to use. For example, we need to go through a process of training and to test our algorithms to make sure they will work the way that we want. This means that we need to split up the data that we have into the training data and the testing data.

These two sets are important to making sure our algorithms are going to work properly. Having them set up and using these sets in the proper manner will help us to get the best results when it comes to working in machine learning. The rules are pretty simple with this, though, so you will be able to get started without any problems along the way.

For example, we need to make sure that the data we are using is high quality to start with. If you do not have enough data or the data is not high in quality, then your algorithm is going to get trained improperly, and will not work the way that you want. Always be careful about the kind of data that you are using in this process

Next, we need to make sure that we are splitting up the data properly. We should have a group for testing and a group for training. Your training set should be much larger to ensure that you are properly training the data that you have and that the algorithm will get a good dose of the examples that you present and what you want it to do.

Training and Testing Your Data

As we go through some of the processes with working on our data and these algorithms, we have to make sure that we are training and testing all of the algorithms first. You can't just write a few lines of code and then put in your data, hoping to get a good prediction to pop out. You need to take the time to train and test the data through that algorithm, to ensure that the accuracy is there, and to make sure that the algorithm is going to be ready for you to work with.

The first step to this is going to be the training of your data. You have to make sure that you are spending a good deal of time training your data so that it knows the right way to behave. Out of the splitting of the data that we did before; you want to have about 75 to 85 percent of your data be in the training set. This ensures that you have enough data there that will help you to really train the algorithm and gives it plenty of time to learn along the way as well.

Then you can feed all of that training data through your algorithm and let it have some time to form those connections and learn what it is supposed to do. From there, you will then need to test the data that you are working with, as well. This will be the rest of the data that you are working with. You can feed this through the algorithm, and wait to see how much accuracy comes back.

Keep in mind with this one that most of the time; these algorithms are going to be able to learn by experience. This means that while they may not have as high accuracy as you would like in the beginning, they will get better. In fact, you may have to go through and do the training and testing phases a few times in order to increase the accuracy enough that you will use the algorithm to make predictions.

You want to get the accuracy as high as possible. However, if you are noticing that the accuracy tends to be lower, and is going below 50 percent, or is not improving as you do some iterations of the training and testing phases, then this is a bad sign. It shows us that you either are not using enough data in your training for the algorithm to properly learn, or you are using bad data that is confusing the algorithm.

This is why we do the training and testing phases. It helps us to catch some of the problems that may happen with this data and will allow us time to make the necessary changes to the data and algorithm before we rely on the future of our company using badly trained algorithms. We can make the adjustments and run the phases again until the accuracy goes up, and we know that we can rely on that data again.

Working with data is going to be a very big part of working with the machine learning projects that we want to handle, we need to be able to learn how to distinguish the different types of data, how to handle the missing data and the outliers, and how to split up the data so that we are able to properly train and test the algorithms that we want to use. When we are able to work with this, we are going to see some great results through our machine learning, and we will then be able to use these predictions and insights to help improve our business.

Chapter 3: Supervised Learning with Regressions

We spent a bit of time in the first chapter looking at what supervised learning is going to be all about, but we need to spend some time looking at the different algorithms that we are able to work with when it comes to this kind of supervised learning. We are going to start out here with some looks at how to work with supervised learning on regression problems, but then we will move on to those that we are able to do with classification problems later on.

Remember that the supervised learning that we will use here is going to be the kind of learning that provides the algorithm with a lot of examples. The input is going to include the corresponding output so that the machine and the system are then able to take a look at the information and learn what the right answers are. This may seem like it is cheating a bit, but the system is able to learn from those examples and then use that information on some of the unseen and new data that it gets later on.

We can find that this is an effective and quick method of working with machine learning, and it can get our algorithms written out pretty quickly. That is why supervised machine learning is going to be used on a regular basis on these kinds of projects. Some of the different options that you are able to use when it comes to supervised learning with regression problems will include:

The Linear Regression

We now need to take a look at what a linear regression is all about. These models are going to show us, or predict the relationship that will show up between two factors or variables. The factor that we are predicting in this model will be the dependent variable. Then the factors that we are using in order to predict the value of the dependent variable will be known as the independent variable.

Good data is not always going to tell us the full story. The regression analysis is going to be used in research as it is able to establish the correlation between variables. But the correlation is not always going to be the same as causation. Even a line that comes up in a simple linear regression that fits well with the points of data may not be able to say something definitive when it is time to look at the cause and effect relationship that is there.

In a simple linear regression like this one, each of the observations that we have will consist of two values. One value is going to be for the dependent variable, and then the other will be the independent variable. In this model, we are going to work with a straight line that will approximate the relationship between these two.

Multiple regression analysis, though, is when we are going to take at least two, and sometimes more, independent variables, and we will use these in a regression analysis. When this happens, the model is no longer going to be a simple linear one for us to work with.

The linear regression is going to have a number of practical uses along the way. Most applications that come with this are going to fall into one of the following broad categories. The first one is to predict or forecast or for error reduction. This can be used to help with a predictive model when it is time to work with an observed set of data values, and the response that comes. After we are able to create this model, if there are some additional values that are collected without the right response to it, the fitted model that we can use is still able to make a prediction for this.

If we have a goal to use this to help explain variation in the response variable that can be attributed to the variation in the explanatory variable, then this kind of analysis is going to be used to quantify the strength that we are able to see between the response and the explanatory variable.

Often we are going to be able to fit the linear regression with the approach of the least squared, but there are other options to work with based on what you are hoping to get out of the process. The least-squares approach can be used to help fit some models that are not always linear. What this means is that the terms of the linear model and least-squares are linked to one another closely; they are not going to be synonymous with one another.

The Cost Function

A cost function is going to be a mathematical formula that we are able to use to help us chart how something is going to change, especially when we look at production expenses at different output levels. The cost function is able to estimate the total cost that we see in production, given the quantity of the product or service that we are producing.

The management of your company is able to use this kind of model in order to run different production scenarios and to help predict what the total cost would be to produce your product, based on the level of output that you are using. The cost function is going to have its own formula to get things done, and this is going to be $C(x) = FC + V(x)$. Ci is going to be the total cost of production the FC is going to be the total costs that are fixed, V is the variable cost, and then x is going to be the number of units.

Understanding the cost unction of a company is going to be helpful in a lot of different scenarios, but especially when it comes to the process of budgeting because it is going to help your management to understand the cost behavior that we are able to see with a product. This is important to help us anticipate the costs that could be incurred in the next operating period at a planned level of activity. It will also allow the management to evaluate how efficient they were with the production process when the operating period is all done.

We can take a look at how to work with this one as well. Let's say that we are going to work with a toy manufacturer and they have asked to have a cost study to make sure they can improve the budget forecasts for the next year. They pay rent that is $300 a month right now, and their electricity is going to come out to $30. Each toy is going to require $5 in plastic and then $2 in cloth.

With this in mind, we are going to figure out how much it is going to cost for the company to manufacture 1200 toys that year, and then compare it to how much it will cost them to manufacture 1500 toys for the year.

The first thing that we need to do to make this work is to figure out which costs are going to be considered fixed, and which ones are the variable costs. The fixed costs are basically going to be any that are incurred, regardless of how much we are manufacturing the toys, and then the variable will be the ones that we have to pay per unit of production. What this means is that the electricity and the rent are going to be fixed, and then the cloth and the plastic are going to be variable costs.

Let's start out with the steps that we would take in order to produce the 12,000 toys a year. This is going to get us the following equation (keep in mind that the fixed cost here is going to be 330 multiplied by 12 so that we can figure out how much the rent and the utilities will be for the whole year.

C (1200) = $3,960 + 1200(5 + 2)
C (1200) = $12,360

But then we are able to take a look at how much it would take in order to do the same thing with 1500 toys. This one is going to use the formula below to help get it done:

C (1500) = $3,960 + 1500(5 + 2)
C (1500) = $14,460

The fixed costs in this on are going to stay the same, no matter how much output we are going to produce. This is why the cost per unit is going to go down or decrease when we make more units. The rent and the utilities will stay the same regardless of how many units we are trying to produce and sell, so usually working with a larger output here is going to give us more in profits for charging the same amount on the products.

Using Weight Training with Gradient Descent

One of the iterative optimization algorithms that we are going to be able to use when we want to find the minimum of a convex function is going to be the gradient descent. This one is going to be based on ideas of calculus, and it is going to really rely on the properties that happen with the first derivative in order to find out in what direction, and even in what magnitude, the coefficients of our function need to be modified along the way. This gradient descent is going to be used when we have some parameters that we are not able to calculate in an analytical manner, and we need to search for it with an optimization algorithm.

Imagine a large container we would use to eat off of, or a big container that we are able to store some fruit in. For our purposes here, the bowl is going to be the cost function or f. A random part on the container is the cost of the current values of your coefficients. We will see that the bottom then is going to be the cost of the coefficients that have the best set and the minimum of the function.

The goal, when using this process, is to try out more than one value for the coefficients, and then evaluate their cost. This will then allow you to go through and select out new coefficients that you can use, ones that have a slightly lower or better cost than the one you were looking at. If you are able to go through and repeat this process enough times, it is going to help us reach the bottom of the container, and then we will know the values of the coefficients that will give us that minimum cost.

There are a few different types of gradient descents that we are able to work with here. The first one is going to be the batch gradient descent for machine learning. The goal of your supervised machine learning is going to be to estimate a target function that is able to map out the input data over to the output variables. This is going to describe all of the regression and classification problems. This is a good look at what the batch gradient descent is all about. This is going to actually be one of the most common forms of gradient descent that we will see in machine learning.

But then we are going to move on to the stochastic gradient descent that is there. These algorithms are going to be slow when you want to run them on some really large sets of data, because one iteration of this kind of algorithm requires that you have a prediction for each instance in training, it can take you a very long time to do this when you have instances that number in the millions.

In these kinds of situations, you can change how you work with the gradient descent and use the stochastic gradient descent. The procedure of a regular descent is going to run, but the update that we see on the coefficients is going to be performed on each instance of training, rather than at the end of the batch of instances. The first step for this is going to require that the order of our set of data for training is going to be random. By mixing up the order that we are doing with these coefficients, we are able to help harness the random walk and make sure that we don't get stuck or distracted.

The updated procedure that we are able to work with this one is going to be the same as the regular gradient descent, but it will not sum out the cost over all of the training patterns. Instead, it is going to be calculated for one training pattern. The learning is going to be faster with this option when we focus on large sets of data.

Polynomial Regression

And finally, we need to take a look at something that is known as the polynomial regression. When we are working with statistics, this kind of regression is going to be one of the analyses of regression that we can work with that will be able to check out the relationship between the dependent and the independent variable and is going to model this relationship as the nth degree polynomial in x. This is going to fit us into a nonlinear relationship between the value that we see with x and the corresponding conditional mean of y.

There are a lot of times when we will use this kind of regression, especially when we want to work with something like the growth rate of tissues, the distribution that we are able to find with carbon isotopes in some of the lake sediments that we see, and the progression of disease epidemics.

Although this regression is going to take some of our nonlinear models and has the data fit it, it is going to be more of a statistical estimation problem. It is going to be linear with the idea that the regression function is going to be linear in some of the unknown parameters that we have with the estimated data. For this reason, it is going to be considered one of the cases of multiple linear regressions.

The independent variables that show up are going to result from the polynomial expansion of the baseline variables, and they are going to be known as higher-degree terms. Such variables can be used when we are doing settings of classification.

There would be times that we would be working with regression problems when it comes to working with machine learning. Adding in some of these regression algorithms can help you to sort through the data that you have in a more efficient manner, and will ensure that you are able to get your data sorted through and find out the predictions and insights that you are looking for as well. Some of the other times when we would want to work with the polynomial regression will include:

1. **When the researcher thinks that there are some relationships that will fit on a curved line. Clearly, these types of cases are going to show us a term that is polynomial.**

2. **When we want to do an inspection of the residuals, if we try to fit a linear model to a data that is curved, then the scatter plot of residuals on the predictor is going to have patches of many positive residuals in the manner. If this does happen, then we can see that this kind of situation is not going to be appropriate for the needs that we have.**

3. **An assumption in the usual multiple linear regression analysis that all of our variables that should be independent are actually this way. in this kind of model, we will find that this is an assumption that is not going to be satisfied at all.**

Basically, we will find that the biggest goal of this kind of analysis of regression is that we want to model the expected value that is going to show up in our dependent variables. We would do this in terms of the value of our independent variable that is going to be x. This will help us to get some of the work that we need to be done when it comes to this kind of regression as well.

Chapter 4: Regularization

To start here, we need to look at some of the foundations of overfitting. Let's assume that you are looking to make some predictions on the price movement of a stock in the future. We then decide to go through and gather up some of the historical daily prices of the stock, maybe going back over the past ten days or so, and then plot the stock price on a scatter plot as we would need. You would then want to go through and capture some of the information about the movements of the stock price. You are then able to assess and gather data for 16 features that you would like to follow because you know the stock price is going to be dependent on them. These are going to include:

1. The competition of the company.
2. The sentiment of the investors
3. The Foreign Exchange Rates
4. The interest rates
5. Inflation rate
6. The future contracts of the company.
7. The current contracts of the company
8. Information on the management of the company
9. The state of the M&A of the company
10. The current and the size of the futures contract of the company.
11. The dividends that the company is able to provide.
12. Any future announcements that the company may release.
13. The profits that the company is making.
14. The earnings of the company.

15. How the industry as a whole is performing at the time.

Once we have been able to gather, clean, scale, and transform the data, it is time to split it out into training and test sets of data. You will need to go through and feed the training data into the model that you chose for machine learning in order to get it trained. After you have had some time to train the algorithms or the models, you can then go through and test out the accuracy that happens with the model by passing through the set of test data.

The goal with this is actually to go through and chart out the prices. You should find that the actual prices of the stocks are going to be random. However, the predicted price of your stock is going to fall into a smooth curve. It has not gone through and fits itself too closely with the training set that you have, and this helps us to work with the generalization of the unseen data better.

Different Types of Fitting with Predicted Prices

We may want to make sure that we want to assume that the plot actual versus the predicted stock prices and we are going to then come up with a few different types of charts along the way:

1. Straight Line to Show Predicted Price

When we have a chart that shows the predicted price in a straight line, this shows us that the algorithm has gone through and has come up with a really strong pre-conception about the data. This is usually a sign that there is a high bias in the information and will show us something known as underfitting. These are not good models to use when you would like to predict new data and should be thrown out in most cases.

2. A Very Strong Closely Fitted Line

This one is an example of the other possible extreme. It may look like it is doing a really good job helping us to predict the price of the stock. However, this is going to be something that is known as overfitting. This is also going to be seen as a high-variance because it has learned the training data in a manner that is so accurate that it will not be able to generalize the information well. This makes it hard to go through and make some predictions on the new and unseen data that is there. These models are also not going to be good when you want to use them to make predictions on the new data.

If we go through with this model and feed it some new data, then you will find that the accuracy of those predictions is going to be really poor. It is also going to be a sign that we are not providing the model with enough data for training. Overfitting is when the model is going to over train itself on the data that you used for this purpose. This could be because we have too many features showing up in the data or because the algorithm has not had time to go through enough data. It is going to happen when the difference that shows up between the predicted values and the actual values is close to 0.

How to Detect Overfitting

Now that we have taken a look at why this overfitting is such a bad thing, it is important for us to go through and figure out when overfitting is going to occur and then figure out how to fit it. The models that you are working with that have been overfitting on the training data will be the ones that are not able to generalize well to the new examples. These are not going to be very good at predicting some of the data that is not seen yet.

This means that when you are trying to add new data to the mix, then you are going to end up with an algorithm that is not doing its job very well. This implies that the model is going to be extremely accurate during training, but when it is time to make predictions on data that it has not seen before, the results are going to be poor overall.

If the measure of accuracy, such as mean error squared, ends up being quite a bit lower when you are working with training the model, and then you see that the accuracy starts to deteriorate on the set of data that you are using for testing, then this is a good sign that overfitting is happening with the data and you may need to supply it with different data, or at least more data, in order to increase the accuracy again.

Often the best way for us to go through with this and figure out whether or not there is overfitting with the data that we want to use, is to chart out the results on a graph. This may seem like we are getting ahead of ourselves, but these visuals will really help us to see some of the complex relationships that are going to show up on our data, and they can tell us almost instantly whether there is an issue with overfitting going on.

When you are working with a particular algorithm, and you are worried about the issue of overfitting, you simply need to go through and plot out the graph. If there is a straight line that shows up on the graph, and all of the points are right on the line, or at least touching the line that is there, then this is a bad sign that overfitting is going on. It is time to go back through and check on the data that you are using, or maybe just do some more training with a wider variety of data, in order to fix this kind of problem.

How Can I Fix Overfitting?

The good news is that there are a few steps that we are able to work in order to help fix some of the issues that come with overfitting. First, we are able to randomly remove some of the features that we are putting into the algorithm, and then use this to help us assess the accuracy of the algorithm in a more iterative manner. However, this can be effective, but the process is slow and can be really tedious. There are going to be four common methods that we are able to use in order to reduce some of the overfittings that we see. Some of these include:

1. **Reduce the features:** The most obvious out of the options that we are able to use is to reduce some of the features. You are able to compute the correlation matrix of our features, and then we can reduce some of the features that happen to be the most highly correlated with one another.

2. **Model selection algorithms:** Another method that we are able to use is going to be the model selection algorithms. These are the algorithms that have the power to choose the features that have the greatest importance and keeps those around, while limiting some of the others that don't seem to affect the data as much The biggest problem that we are going to see with this one is that it is possible to lose out on some valuable information at times.

3. **Feed-in more data:** We can also take a look at feeding in more data to the model. Sometimes this is all that we need in order to handle some of the issues that come with overfitting. You should aim in training a set to feed in enough

data to the models so that you are able to train, test, and validate the model thoroughly. For example, you should do about 60 percent of your data to help train the model, 20 percent to test the data, and then 20 to help validate the model that you are working with.

We need to explore the idea of regularization a bit more. The aim of this is to help keep all of the features, but then impose a constraint on the magnitude of the coefficients that you are able to get. This is often seen as the preferred method because you do not have to lose out on any of your features because you are busy penalizing them like some of the other methods. When the constraints are applied to the parameters, then the model is going to end up not overfitting as much because it can produce a smooth function.

The parameters that we work within regularization, which are going to be known as the penalty factors, are going to be able to introduce which controls the parameters and will ensure that the model is not going to over train itself on any of the training data that you are working with. We will also find that these parameters are going to be at smaller values to help eliminate the issue of overfitting. When the coefficients work with larger values, then the regularization parameters are going to penalize some of the optimization functions that are there.

While we are on regularization, we should look at the two most common techniques that we are able to work with on this. The first one is going to be Lasso. This is going to be a tool for feature selection, and it is going to be able to help us eliminate any of the features that not important to what we are doing. It can also add in a penalty, which is going to be the absolute of the magnitude that we will see with the coefficient.

What this is going to do is ensure that the features we are working with are not going to end up applying some high weights to the prediction that comes with our algorithm. The result of this is that some of the weights are going to turn into zero. This means that the data of some of our features are not going to be seen as important at all, and they will not be used in the algorithm that we have at all.

And the second technique that works here is going to be a ridge. This one is a bit different but can still have a lot of the features and strengths that we need. With ridge, we are going to add in a penalty, which is going to be the square of the magnitude of the coefficients. As a result of this, you will find that some of the weights that we have are going to end up being close to 0. This is a good way to smooth out some of the effects that we will see on the features as well.

Overfitting our data is something that can be a big issue when we are working with machine learning. We want to get accurate information out of what we are doing in this process, and if the algorithm ends up overfitting, then it is not guessing the data very well. It may do well with the training data that we are working with, but it is not going to do all that well when it comes to taking on new data, and that is when you really need this algorithm to work its best.

Following some of the techniques that we have in this chapter, and learning how this overfitting occurs in the first place, is going to be one of the important first steps that you can follow in order to make sure that this issue doesn't happen - the more that you are able to prevent this from happening, the more accurate and efficient your models will end up being in machine learning. When we can keep underfitting and overfitting from happening with some of the data that we have, we are going to get amazing results, and our models will work in the manner that we want.

Chapter 5: Supervised Learning with Classification

Supervised machine learning is going to be one of the algorithms that you will use a lot in machine learning because there are a lot of applications. This is a good and effective method of teaching your machine on algorithms and how you would like it to behave. This is because this method is going to show the algorithm all of the examples, with their corresponding answers, right from the beginning, making sure that the algorithm is able to learn the right way faster than before.

This is why there are going to be so many different types of supervised machine learning models and algorithms that we are able to work with. They may take a bit more time in the beginning, but when we use classification and some of the other tools that are out there to help us get it all done, we will find that it is easier to train and test out our models and get some good results in the process. Some of the different supervised machine learning algorithms that we are able to focus on with classification will include:

Logistic Regression

The next algorithm on the list that we need to take a look at is going to be the logistic regression. These are going to be able to help us out with a lot of different problems that we want the data to solve, and if we are able to use it in the right manner, we are going to be able to see some amazing results in the process. As time passed, it started to be used for applications in the social sciences. Logistic regression, though, no matter how we decide to work with it, is going to be used when the target, or our dependent variable, is categorical.

This means that we may use it for a few different situations, such as when we would like to predict whether or not an email that comes to us is spam, or whether or not a tumor is malignant.

To help us see how this goes, we can start with a scenario where we would like to determine whether or not an email that we see is spam or not. If we use linear regression for this instance, we would need to set up a basis wherewith to base our classification with.

From this example alone, it is easy to see that the linear regression is going to fail a bit when it comes to some of the classification problems. Linear regression is not going to be bounded, and this is why we need to work with logistic regression for some of our problems. With this one, the value is going to range from 0 to 1, and nothing in between.

Now, we may see that there are a few different types of logistic regression that we are able to work with. The three main types that we are able to focus our attention on here are going to include:

1. The binary logistic regression: This is going to be a response that is categorical and has only two outcomes possible. When we are looking at emails, for example, it is going to tell us whether the specific email is spam or not.

2. Multinomial logistic regression: This is when there are three or more categories that show up without any order. For example, we may see this one when predicting which food is preferred more such as Vegan, Non-Vegan, and Vegan.

3. Ordinal logistic regression: This is when there are at least three categories, bust sometimes more, to the ordering. For example, we could have a movie rating that goes from one to five.

To help make it easier to predict which class our data is going to belong to, we are going to set a threshold in the beginning. Based on what this threshold is about, the obtained estimated probability is going to be classified into classes. Going back to the idea of the spam earlier, we could have our predicted value be at or above 0.5. When an email reaches this threshold, then the email is going to be seen as spam. If it does not, then it is not seen as spam.

The decision boundary that we are able to work with is going to be seen as non-linear or linear. If preferred the Polynomial order can be changed to get to a more varied boundary if we would prefer. This would give us the variation that we would need.

When we work with the logistical regression, we will find that there are a lot of the other parts we have talked about in this guidebook so far that they are going to show up in the code. This is because there are often times when we need to combine together more than one option when it comes to working with these algorithms. A good way to see some of this is to look at an example of the coding that is needed to work on the logistical regression, and we can see that below:

```
def weightInitialization(n_features):
w = np.zeros((1,n_features))
b = 0
return w,bdef sigmoid_activation(result):
final_result = 1/(1+np.exp(-result))
return final_result
def model_optimize(w, b, X, Y):
m = X.shape[0]

#Prediction
final_result = sigmoid_activation(np.dot(w,X.T)+b)
Y_T = Y.T
```

```
cost = (-1/m)*(np.sum((Y_T*np.log(final_result)) +
((1-Y_T)*(np.log(1-final_result)))))
#

#Gradient calculation
dw = (1/m)*(np.dot(X.T, (final_result-Y.T).T))
db = (1/m)*(np.sum(final_result-Y.T))

grads = {"dw": dw, "db": db}


return grads, costdef model_predict(w, b, X, Y,
learning_rate, no_iterations):
costs = []
for i in range(no_iterations):
#
grads, cost = model_optimize(w,b,X,Y)
#
dw = grads["dw"]
db = grads["db"]
#weight update
w = w - (learning_rate * (dw.T))
b = b - (learning_rate * db)
#
```

```
if (i % 100 == 0):

costs.append(cost)

#print("Cost after %i iteration is %f" %(i, cost))


#final parameters

coeff = {"w": w, "b": b}

gradient = {"dw": dw, "db": db}


return coeff, gradient, costsdef predict(final_pred, m):

y_pred = np.zeros((1,m))

for i in range(final_pred.shape[1]):

if final_pred[0][i] > 0.5:

y_pred[0][i] = 1

return y_pred
```

Many times the logistical regression is going to be a
better choice to go with compared to the linear
regression. This is because this will allow us to catch
some of the instances that are going to be missed, like
what is going to happen with the linear regression.

Multiclass Classification

While we are here, we also need to take a look at some of the benefits of working with the multiclass classification. Classification problems are often going to come with many classes, and there is going to be an imbalanced kind of dataset that will present a different challenge compared to what we see with some of the classification problems. Sometimes the skewed distribution is going to make some of the other algorithms with machine learning less effective, especially when it comes to predicting minority class examples.

We will find that with a multiclass classification problem, you are going to be handling a task of classification that has three or more classes to work with. This means that we could do something like classifying a set of images of fruits, which may be things like pears, apples, and oranges, and some other fruits if you would like to add these in as well.

This kind of classification is going to make some assumptions in order to make sure that things are going to happen. For example, it will make one assumption that each of the samples is going to be assigned to one and no more than one label. For example, fruit can be either a pear or an apple, but it is not possible for this fruit to be both at the same time.

While some of the classification algorithms that are out there are naturally going to be set up to permit the use of more than two of these classes, others are going to be binary algorithms instead, and these can also be turned into multinomial classifiers with a lot of different strategies along the way. One thing to remember with this one though is that we should not confuse this kind of classification should not be confused with the idea of multi-label classification, where the multiple labels are to be predicted for each instance.

There are many times when we are going to work with the classification problems, especially when it comes to handling things with supervised machine learning. These can make it easier to split up some of the different algorithms that you have and will ensure that you are able to see what classes are there, and how to understand some of the data that you have available.

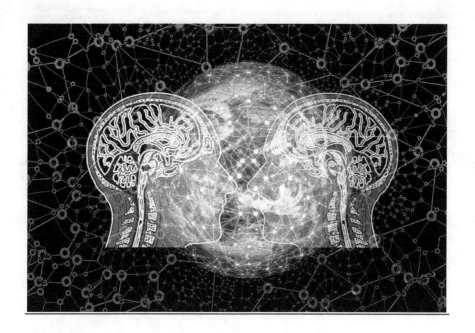

Chapter 6: Non-linear Classification Models

There are a lot of things that we are able to do when it is time to work with some of the classification problems that we have along the way. These are really useful when it is time to work through some of the data that we have, and they can often be one of the best ways that we are able to learn about the data, see which groups the data falls into, and so much more. Some of the other classification models that you are able to work with, the ones that do not fit in with

the linear classification models, will include some of
the following:

K-Nearest Neighbor

The first option that we are going to look at when it comes to working on the non-linear classification models will include the K-Nearest Neighbor or the KNN algorithm. This is going to be an example of a supervised machine learning algorithm, so we will need to have some labeled data in place as well.

There are a few benefits that you will see when it is time to work with the KNN algorithm. When we are working with the algorithm, it is helpful for us to cut down the noise that may be in the set of data. Depending on the data that we are working with, you may find that the noise is going to be really loud, and making sure the noise is gone going to ensure that we are able to handle the work as well and get more accurate results in the process.

There are many algorithms that we are able to work with when it comes to working with machine learning. This makes it hard to know why you would want to work with this kind of algorithm over some of the others. The benefits of working with the KNN algorithm and why you would want to choose it over some of the other options include:

1. It can work well with problems, even if they are considered multi-class.

2. You are able to apply this algorithm to both problems that are regressive and those that are classification.

3. There aren't any assumptions that come up with the data. This ensures that you get the information that you want, rather than having any assumptions in the place, causing some issues.

4. It is an easy algorithm to work with. It is easy to understand, especially if you are brand new to the machine learning process.

However, there are more options for algorithms that you are able to work with because the KNN algorithm isn't going to be perfect in each and every situation that you go to. Some of the negatives that come with using the KNN algorithm include:

1. It is going to be computationally and memory intensive expensive. If you don't have the right system and the right amount of space to work with, it is going to make it more difficult to see the results that you want from this algorithm.

2. If there are a lot of independent variables that you are going to work with, you will find that the KNN algorithm is going to struggle.

3. The KNN algorithm isn't going to work that well if you have any rare event, or skewed, target variables.

4. Sensitive to the scale of data.

For any of the problems that we are going to work with, you will find that having a smaller value of k is going to give us more variance in any of the predictions that we are working with. In addition, when you set it so that k is at a bigger value, it is possible that there is going to be more bias in the model as you work on it too.

While you are working with this one, though, there may be times when you will need to go through and create some dummy variables. This is going to make it easier to figure out the categorical variables that will show up in this algorithm. This is different than the regressions that we will look for though because you can work with creating the k dummies rather than just the k-1.

With this in mind, we need to take a look at the best way to handle finding these k values in the first place. This is often done with the use of cross-validation. It is going to be important to use this process in order to estimate what the error of validation will be. To make this happen, we will need to hold out a subset of the training set from the process of building up the model.

Cross-validation is going to involve us going through and dividing up our training data randomly. We are going to work with a 10 fold validation, so that means we would want to divide up the training sets that we have into 10 groups. We want to keep them as close to the same in size as possible as we go through the dividing. From this, 90 percent of our data is going to be the kind that we use to train our model. The other ten percent or so will be used to help validate the model that we are working with and to test whether or not it is working.

The misclassification rate that we need to focus on for this one is going to be computed when we look at the ten percent that you saved back for the validation. This procedure is going to need to go through and repeat itself ten times because of how we are doing all of this. Each of the groups of observations that we run into is going to be seen as validation, and then you can test it as well.

Decision Trees and Random Forests

Often, the decision tree and the random forest are going to work together. These are going to be efficient tools of data that will help you to take two of the choices that you would like to work with, especially when the choices are very different, and then will use this information in order to help you pick out which decision is the best for your needs so that you can grow your business and more.

When you are presented with more than one option, and they all look like they are good options to work with, the decision tree is going to be a good option to choose along the way. These will help you to take some of these choices and then see what the possible outcomes may be with these, making it easier to figure out what is the best course of action to take.

Now, you will find that there are a few different ways that you are able to work with these decision trees. Many of those who are working with machine learning will use it if either of their variables is categorical, and one is random. However, there are times when you will need to use these decision trees with some of the classification problems that you have. To ensure that you are picking out and creating your decision tree well, then you need to make sure that you take all of the sets of data that you have and then split them up to be in two or more sets, with some similar data in each one. You can then sort this out with the help of independent variables because it will help you to set it up the way that the decision tree needs.

Sometimes the decision tree is not to be what we need, and we will find that it is better to have more than one decision tree to get the work that we want. This is when the decision tree is going to be turned over to a random forest. These are popular to work with because they allow you to look at many possible, decisions that you want to make, and come up with the one that you would like to work with. So, the best way to think about these random forests is that they are going to be a bunch of different decision trees that are going to work together.

There are going to be many applications of using the random forest. This is because the random forest is perfect most of the time, it is going to do a better job of providing you with some insights and predictions than some of the other algorithms. Some of the ways that you are able to use these forests and make sure that they will benefit you include:

- When you are working on your own training sets, you will find that all of the objects that are inside a set will be generated randomly, and it can be replaced if your random tree things that this is necessary and better for your needs.
- If there are M input variable amounts, then $m<M$ is going to be specified from the beginning, and it will be held as a constant. The reason that this is so important because it means that each tree that you have is randomly picked from their own variable using M.

- The goal of each of your random trees will be to find the split that is the best for the variable m.

- As the tree grows, all of these trees are going to keep getting as big as they possibly can. Remember that these random trees are not going to prune themselves.

- The forest that is created from a random tree can be great because it is much better at predicting certain outcomes. It is able to do this for you because it will take all prediction from each of the trees that you create and then will be able to select the average for regression or the consensus that you get during classification.

Random forests are a good tool that a programmer is able to use when they would like to make sure that they add in some data science to the machine learning that you are doing, and there are going to be many benefits. But any time that you are looking for an easy way to look through some of the options that are available for your work, and you want help making some smart decisions, then the decision trees and random forests will be the best option for you to choose.

Working with Support Vector Machines

We can also spend some time working with the support vector machines, or SVM. These are going to be there to help us take each set of the data and then plot them so that they will show up on one n-dimensional of N. N is going to be the number of features that you would like to work with all of this. You will then be able to take the value of the features and work to translate this over to the value that you will need for your chosen coordinates. The job that you are able to do when it is time to reach this point is to figure out where your hyperplane will fall because this is going to be the part that will show you what differences are there between the classes that show up.

Here you may notice that it is possible that more than one support vector is going to show up. The good news is that many of these are obviously not going to be important, and they are just going to be the coordinates of the individual observations that you are going to see here. Then you are able to work with the

SVM to turn into your frontier, the part that is able to separate these parts into classes, and then there will be the line and the hyperplane, which are the two parts that we need to focus on the most.

Up to this point, some of the work that we are looking at will seem a bit confusing. But there are a few steps that we are able to follow in order to really find out how to sort this data and use the SVM for our needs. First, we need to look for our own hyperplane. One thing that you will notice is that this algorithm is going to bring out more than one hyperplane that we can focus on. This is a challenge for beginners because you want to make sure that the hyperplane you pick is going to be the best one for sorting through the data and making it work for your needs.

The good thing to remember here is that even if you do have a few options when it comes to hyperplanes, there are still going to be some easy steps that we are able to use to help us pick out the right one. The specific steps that you are able to use when trying to figure out the hyperplane for your SVM will include:

- We are going to start out with three hyperplanes that we will call 1, 2, and 3. Then we are going to spend time figuring out which hyperplane is right so that we can classify the star and the circle.

- The good news is there is a pretty simple rule that you can follow so that it becomes easier to identify which hyperplane is the right one. The hyperplane that you want to go with will be the one that segregates your classes the best.

- That one was easy to work with, but in the next one, our hyperplanes of 1, 2, and 3 are all going through the classes, and they segregate them in a manner that is similar. For example, all of the lines or these hyperplanes are going to run parallel with each other. From here you may find that it is hard to pick which hyperplane is the right one.

- For the issue that is above, we will need to use what is known as the margin. This is basically the distance that occurs between the hyperplane and the nearest data point from either of the two classes. Then you will be able to get some numbers that can help you out. These numbers may be closer together, but

they will point out which hyperplane is going to
be the best.

The Neural Networks

We would be working with the Scikit-Learn library in this process of machine learning, and one that can handle a lot of really things for machine learning will be the neural networks. These are used quite a bit because they will work similar to the human brain, picking up on different patterns and more, and forming stronger connections each time that something is correct with its predictions.

When we are working with these neural networks, we will find that there are often a lot of layers, and each of these layers is going to be spending time to see whether there are some patterns there are not. If the network is able to find that new pattern, then they will go on through to the next layer. And this process will continue until there are no more patterns for the process to find, and until we are done and the neural network is able to make some predictions as well.

There are a few things that will happen at this point, based on how the program works. If the algorithm went through the process above and was able to sort through all of the different layers, it will then make a prediction. If that prediction is right, the neurons in the system will turn out stronger than ever. This is because the program has used artificial intelligence in order to make some strong associations between the patterns and the object. The more times that the system can come back with the right answer, the more efficient it will be when you turn it on and use it again.

Now, this may seem a little bit farfetched, but a closer examination of these neural networks will help us to see how they work together and why they are so important. For our example, let's say that your goal is to create a program that is able to take a picture that you input into it, and then, by looking at that picture and going through the layers, the program is able to recognize that the image in that picture is that of a car.

If the program has been set up in the proper manner, it is going to make the right prediction that there is a car in the picture. The program is able to come up with this prediction based on some of the features that it already knows belongs to the car, including the color, the number on the license plate, the placement of the doors, the headlights, and more.

With this one, we need to make sure to remember there is the potential for many layers to show up, but the good news is that the more layers we are able to go through with our images, the more accurate the predictions are going to be overall. If your neural network can make some accurate predictions, then it is going to be able to learn this lesson and will hold onto it along the way and will get faster and more efficient at making the predictions later on.

The neat thing that happens when we are working with these neural networks is that they are able to remember some of the work that they have done in the past. So, if you present the neural network with a picture of a car, and it makes the prediction that the image in that picture is a car, it will remember this information later, similar to what the human mind can do.

Then, if you present it with a picture of a car, especially if this new image is similar to the one that you showed to the algorithm earlier, it is going to remember what it learned before. The algorithm will get through the various layers of the image really quickly and can give a prediction of a car in much less time than before. And this process continues on, with the neural networks getting better at predictions the more times that it is able to go through the information and try out its skills. Just think about all of the ways that we would be able to work with this kind of technology, and this algorithm, to get some of our machine learning algorithms done and taken care of.

Chapter 7: Validation and Optimization Techniques

Now that we have taken a look at a few of the different algorithms that go with machine learning, it is time for us to take a look at some of the ways that we can make these algorithms a little bit better. We would be looking at the validation of the algorithm to make sure that it is working the way that we want, and then, we will focus on how to optimize the techniques that we are working on so that we get the best predictions and insights that we are able to get out of those algorithms. So, let's dive in and see what we are able to do with some of these techniques to make them work for our needs.

Cross-Validation Techniques

The first validation technique that we need to work with is known as the cross-validation technique. We are going to work on our machine learning algorithms here, and at the same time, we are going to take our set of data and divide it into three parts. We are going to have the set for training, the set for validation, and the set for testing.

The training set is the first one that we will look at. This is the one that we are going to use to help train the model. We will want to put about 60 percent of the data that we have available to work on training the model to make sure that it is ready to go.

Then we are going to work with the data set that handles the validation. Once we have been able to select out a model that can perform well with the training set, it is time to run the model with our validation set. This is going to be a small subset of the data, and it is usually going to range from 10 to 20 percent of the data that you have. This set is going to help us with these models because it is going to give us an evaluation, without bias, of the fitness of the model. If the error on the data set for validation increases, then it is possible that we are working with a model that overfits.

And finally, we have the test data set. This is going to be new data that has never been used in training at all. This is going to be a bit smaller, but it is going to contain about 5 to 20 percent of the set of data that we have, and it is meant to help us test out the model evaluation that we are working on to see whether it is accurate or not.

In some cases, there is going to be training and a test set, and the programmer is not going to work with any validation set. There are some issues with this one, though. Due to the sample variability between the test set and the training, the model is going to provide us with a better prediction on the data that we train but will fail to generalize on the test data. This can make us deal with a low error rate during training, but a high rate of an error on the testing phase of this process.

When we go through and split out the set of data that we have into training, test, and validation set, we are going to work with just a subset of data, and then we will know when it is possible to train on fewer observations of the model are not going to perform well, and then we will see that it is going to give us an overestimated test error rate.

To help us solve both of these issues, we are going to work with cross-validation. This is technique involves partitioning the data so that it all goes into subsets. This allows us to train the data on one of the subsets, and then we will use the other one to help us to evaluate the performance of the model that we are working with as well.

To help us out here and to make sure that we reduce how much variability shows up in our data, we may go through and perform many rounds of this cross-validation, but we are going to do this with different subsets of the same data. We can then combine the validation results form these rounds in order to come up with a good estimate of the predictive performance that we are going to be able to get from that model. The cross-validation then is going to provide us with an estimate of the performance of the model that is more accurate than just training once and then assuming it is all going to work.

With this in mind, there are going to be a few different techniques that we are able to see with cross-validation, and these are going to include:

1. Leave one out cross-validation or LOOCV: In this one, we are going to take our set of data and divide it into two pairs to work on. In the first part, we are going to have a single observation, which is going to be the test data. And then, in the second one, we are going to have all of the other observations that come in our set of data, and these will form up our training data.

   a. There are a few advantages to working with this one. First, we are going to find that there is far less bias because we are going to use all of the set of data for training compared to some of the validation set approach where we are only working with part of the data to help with training.

b. There isn't going to be any randomness in the training or the test data because we will perform this many times, and it will still give us the same results.

c. There are some disadvantages that come with this one as well. For example, MSE is going to vary as the test data is going to work with just one single observation. This sometimes adds some variability to work. If the data point that you work with ends up being an outlier, then you will find that the variability is going to be much higher.

d. The execution of this model is going to be more expensive than some other options because the model has to be fitted n times rather than just once or twice.

2. K Fold cross-validation: This is going to be a technique of cross-validation that is going to take the set of data and randomly divide it into k groups or folds that are similar in size. The first fold that you have is going to be used for testing, and then the model is going to be trained on k-1 folds. The process is going to be repeated K amount of times, and each time that you do, this will have a different group of the data that you will use for validation.

a. There are a few advantages that come with this one. First, the computation time is going to be reduced as we go through the process 10 times, or less, depending on what value you give to k.

b. This one is also going to have a reduced bias, so you can rely on the information that you have more.

c. Every point of data gets to be tested just once and is used in training the k-1 times.

d. The variance of the resulting estimate is going to be reduced the number of times that k increases.

e. There are some disadvantages of k fold or the 10-old cross-validation. The training algorithm, compared to some of the other options, is going to be computationally intensive because the algorithm has to start over again and rerun from scratch k times to be effective.

3. Then we can work with the stratified cross-validation. This is a technique where we rearrange the data in a manner that each fold is going to be a proper representation of the set of data it is going to force the process so that each fold has to have at least m instances of each class. This type of approach is going to ensure that one class of data will not be over-represented, especially when the variable you are using as the target is not balanced well.

   a. For example, we may work on a binary classification problem where we would like to predict if a person on the Titanic was a survivor or not. We are going to have two classes here; the passenger either survives or doesn't survive. We will then ensure that each fold is going to have a percentage of passengers who survived, and another percentage of the passengers who did not make it.

4. The time-series cross-validation: Splitting up the time series that you have in a random manner is not going to help out as much because the time-related data is going to get all messed up. If we are working on predicting the prices of the stocks and then we randomly split up the data, this is just going to make things difficult. This is why we would want to work with a time series cross-validation. In this one, each day is going to be a test data, and then we would consider the data that we had from the day before as part of our training set.

    a. We can start by training out the model with a minimum number of observations, and then we will use the data for the next day to help test the data. And we keep moving through this set of data. This will ensure that we are able to consider the time-series aspect that comes with this prediction.

Hyperparameter Optimization

One thing that we need to spend a bit of time looking at is the idea of hyperparameters. These are properties that are specific to the model that we are working with, ones that are going to be fixed even before we have a chance to train or test the data that we have with the model.

We are able to see one of these examples when we are working with a random forest. The hyperparameter is going to include the number of decision trees that we are able to find in our forest to start with. When working with the neural network, there is going to be a learning rate, the number of layers that are hidden, the number of units that we would like to see come with each layer, and a variety of other parameters along the way.

When we bring up the topic of hyperparameter tuning, we are talking about nothing outside of searching for the right set of hyperparameters in order to achieve the high precision and accuracy that we want. When we optimize these hyperparameters, it is going to end up being one of the trickiest and often one of the hardest parts of building a model up with machine learning.

The main aim that a programmer is going to have when it comes to tuning their hyperparameters is to find the sweet spot. This sweet spot in the parameters of the model is important because it ensures that we are able to get the best performance on our project as possible. There are going to be a few techniques that we can use for the parameter tuning, but we are going to focus on the grid search and the random search in the next section because these are the most widely-used options for parameter optimizing.

Grid and Random Search

The final thing that we are going to focus on in this chapter is the idea of the grid search versus the random search. This will help us to figure out which of the two is going to be better for the work that we want to accomplish. Before we look too much into this though, we need to review the hyperparameter optimization that we talked about earlier, because this is going to be important to some of the work that we are trying to do in this section.

First, we are going to take a look at grid searching. This is where we are going to try every combination of a present list of values of the hyperparameters, and then we are going to do an evaluation of the model with each of these combinations. The pattern that we will follow on this one is going to be similar to what we are able to see with a grid because each of the values is going to be placed into the matrix. Each set of parameters can then be taken into consideration, and we will note the accuracy. Once all of the combinations are evaluated, the model that has the set of parameters that provides us with the most accurate overall is considered the best one to work with.

While this is still a pretty straightforward option to work with, one of the biggest issues that we are going to face with it is when it comes to dimensionality; it is going to suffer when the number of these parameters starts to grow. With as few as four parameters in place, the problem can almost be impractical because the number of evaluations that we need to try to work on with this strategy is going to increase. And when we add in more of these parameters, the dimensionality is just going to make the problem worse.

There are times when we are going to use the grid search, but keep in mind that there are times when it is going to take too long and be too complex. This is when we will work with a random search. This is going to be a technique where some of the random combinations of the hyperparameter are going to be used to help us find the best solution for the model that we have built.

In many cases, this search is going to go through the information and will try out some combinations that are random for the range of values. To help optimize this random search, the function is going to be evaluated at some number of random configurations of the parameter space, as well.

The chances of finding an optimal parameter that you can use are going to be quite a bit higher with the random search because the pattern is going to be rained on the optimized parameters without needing to know any aliases. Random search is going to work the best when we have lower-dimensional data since the time that is taken to find the right set for this is going to be less when you have less iteration to work with.

In many cases, the random search is going to be the best technique here, especially when we have fewer dimensions to work with. There are going to be many practical and theoretical concerns when evaluating these strategies. The strategy that is best for your particular problem, though, is going to be one that finds the best value for the fastest and with the fewest function evaluations and it is possible that this is going to vary one problem to the next.

While it is less common in machine learning than the grid search, this random search is going to show us that we are able to get equal, and sometimes better, values compared to the grid search within fewer evaluations of the functions for some of the problems that we try to work with. You have to decide which method you think is the best for the kind of project that you want to work with at the time.

Chapter 8: Unsupervised Machine Learning with Clustering

Unsupervised machine learning is going to be able to help us out with a variety of problems as we handle some of our algorithms. There are times when we need to go through and sort some of the data we have, and we want to be able to make the machine do the work. Being able to handle clustering is a great way to work with unsupervised machine learning because this ensures that we are able to really see where some of our data points lie and can show us some of the hidden insights and predictions and patterns that are there, many of which we did not know about ahead of time. Some of the unsupervised machine learning options that you can do along with clustering will include:

K-Means Clustering

The first type of unsupervised machine learning that works with clustering is going to be the K-means clustering. This clustering is a good way to take care of all the different data points that we have, and see where they are going to be grouped together. You can choose how many groups of clusters you would like. If you are working with separating your customers into genders, then you may only have two clusters. But when you are working with the ages of the customers or even the geographic regions of the customers, then you may end up with five or more clusters.

The idea that comes with this one is that any of the data points that are in the same cluster are going to be closely related to one another. They are not going to have a lot of similarities to the other points that are in the other clusters that you have. This is important because it allows us to see where all of the points of data are going to be placed and will ensure that we are going to see the best results with this in no time at all.

One place where you may see this data clustering happening is when we are working with data mining. This data mining will really work with the clustering if it is more exploratory in nature. You can also work with clustering in other fields based on what we are trying to find out, such as with pattern recognition, lots of machine learning, image analysis, and computer graphics.

The K-Means clustering algorithm is going to form some clusters in your data based on how similar the data values will be. You can then go through and specify what you would like the value of K to be. The value of K is basically going to be the number of clusters that you would like to separate your data out into. The algorithm will be able to help you from here by selecting the center point for your clusters so that the data points fit in.

Then there are going to be three steps that the algorithm will need to go through including:

1. You will want to start with the Euclidian distance between each data instance and the centroids for all of the clusters.

2. Assign the instances of data to the cluster of centroid with the nearest distance possible.

3. Calculate the new centroid values, depending on the mean values of the coordinates of the data instances from the corresponding cluster.

To work with this kind of process, we have to make sure that we can go through and figure out how many clusters we would like to have in the first place. This helps to tell the algorithm where to place all of your data points, and when you print off the visual that goes with this, you will find that it can really help you to see where the data is going to fall, and how all of the different points are meant to go with one another as well. You may even be able to look at this to find a new cluster, and figure out a new market or a new customer base to organize with as well.

There are a lot of different things that we are able to do when it comes to working with the K-means clustering algorithm, but one of the things that we are going to spend some time looking at here is information and the codes that we need to focus on in order to figure out and add in the soft k-means to our code.

Now that we know a bit about the k-means algorithm in general, and we know some of the different ways that we are able to make this work for our needs, it is time to actually take some of these skills and use some Python code in order to make this algorithm work in machine learning. And implementing the soft k-means and the code that we will have below is one of the best ways to make this happen.

To get started with this process, we need to make sure that we start out with some of the standard imports and libraries that are needed, and that we have the utility functions in place as well. This is important because it is going to help us to get something similar to the Euclidean distance, and the cost function going together. The syntax of Python code that we are able to use with this one will include the following:

```
import numpy as np
import matplotlib.pyplot as plt


def d(u, v):
```

```
    diff = u - v
    return diff.dot(diff)


def cost(X, R, M):
    cost = 0
    for k in xrange(len(M)):
        for n in xrange(len(X)):
            cost += R[n,k]*d(M[k], X[n])
    return cost
```

After this part, we are going to take the time to define your function so that it is able to run the k-means algorithm before plotting the result. This is going to end up with a scatter plot where the color will represent how much of the membership is inside of a particular cluster. We would do that with the following code.

```
def plot_k_means(X, K, max_iter=20, beta=1.0):
    N, D = X.shape
    M = np.zeros((K, D))
```

```
R = np.ones((N, K)) / K

# initialize M to random
for k in xrange(K):
    M[k] = X[np.random.choice(N)]

grid_width = 5
grid_height = max_iter / grid_width
random_colors = np.random.random((K, 3))
plt.figure()

costs = np.zeros(max_iter)
for i in xrange(max_iter):
    # moved the plot inside the for loop
    colors = R.dot(random_colors)
    plt.subplot(grid_width, grid_height, i+1)
    plt.scatter(X[:,0], X[:,1], c=colors)

    # step 1: determine assignments / resposibilities
    # is this inefficient?
    for k in xrange(K):
        for n in xrange(N):
```

```python
        R[n,k] = np.exp(-beta*d(M[k], X[n])) /
np.sum( np.exp(-beta*d(M[j], X[n])) for j in
xrange(K) )

        # step 2: recalculate means
        for k in xrange(K):
            M[k] = R[:,k].dot(X) / R[:,k].sum()

        costs[i] = cost(X, R, M)
        if i > 0:
            if np.abs(costs[i] - costs[i-1]) < 10e-5:
                break

    plt.show()

def main():
    # assume 3 means
    D = 2 # so we can visualize it more easily
    s = 4 # separation so we can control how far apart
the means are
    mu1 = np.array([0, 0])
    mu2 = np.array([s, s])
    mu3 = np.array([0, s])
```

```
N = 900 # number of samples
X = np.zeros((N, D))
X[:300, :] = np.random.randn(300, D) + mu1
X[300:600, :] = np.random.randn(300, D) + mu2
X[600:, :] = np.random.randn(300, D) + mu3


# what does it look like without clustering?
plt.scatter(X[:,0], X[:,1])
plt.show()


K = 3 # luckily, we already know this
plot_k_means(X, K)


# K = 5 # what happens if we choose a "bad" K?
# plot_k_means(X, K, max_iter=30)


# K = 5 # what happens if we change beta?
# plot_k_means(X, K, max_iter=30, beta=0.3)



if __name__ == '__main__':
    main()
```

Hierarchal Clustering

Along the same idea is the K-Means clustering, we also need to take a look at a method that is known as the hierarchal clustering. In statistics and data mining, this is going to be a method of analyzing clusters, where we are going to work to build up a hierarchy of clusters. There are going to be a few strategies that we are able to use to handle this kind of clustering, but often they are going to fall into one of two types, including:

1. **Divisive**: This is going to be the top-down approach. This will include how all of the observations that you are using will start out in one cluster, and then these will be split up and move down through the hierarchy until you reach the end.

2. **Agglomerative**: This one is going to be the opposite. You will start out with each observation falling in its own cluster, and then you are able to merge together pairs of the

clusters as you go up the hierarchy that you are working with.

For the most part, you will be able to determine the splits and the merges in a greedier manner. The results of this are usually going to be presented with a dendrogram.

To help us determine which ones are going to be combined or split up, we need to be able to look for and measure out the dissimilarity between the sets of observations that we are working with. The good news is that with most methods of this kind of clustering, we are going to be able to make this happen with an appropriate metric, which is a measure of distance between observations and pairs, and a linkage criterion that is going to let us know the dissimilarity of sets as a function of the pairwise distances of observations in the sets we are working with.

DBSCAN

DBSCAN is stands for Density-based spatial clustering of applications with noise. This is going to be a pretty well-known data clustering algorithm that is going to be used in things like data mining and machine learning to help us to move our data into clusters so that we are able to read through it and understand better. Based on a set of points, this algorithm is going to be able to group together points that are close to one another based on some kind of distance measurement and a minimum point amount. It is also going to mark out some of the outliers that we have that are found in some of the lower-density regions to help us see where these outliers are.

To keep it simple, we will find that this kind of algorithm is going to come with 2 parameters that we need to know. These are going to include:

1. Eps: This is going to tell us how close the points need to be to one another before they can be

seen as part of the cluster. However, if the distance between the two is either low or even equal, these would be considered as neighbors.

2. minPoints: This is going to be the minimum number of points that are needed to form a region that is dense. So if we set this parameter to 5, then we need to have at least five of these points in order to form a dense region.

Then we are able to move on to doing parameter estimation. This is going to be something that we need to focus on for every kind of task in data mining. To choose the right parameters, we have to understand how they are used and then have at least a basic previous knowledge about the set of data that we are going to work with.

For the eps from above, if the value that you choose is too small, then you will end up with a lot of your data not being clustered. It is going to be considered outliers because it won't be able to provide the points. On another point, if the value that was chosen is too high, clusters will merge, and the majority of objects are going to fall into the same cluster. This means that we need to choose the eps based on the distance of the set of data, but in general, going with a smaller value for this is going to be preferable.

We can also work with the minPoints that we talked about before. As a rule, the minimum of this can be derived when we take the data set as minPoints greater than or equal to D + 1. Larger values are often going to be better for the sets of data that have a lot of noise and will form more significant clusters. The minimum value for the minPoints must be three, but larger the set of data, the larger the value that should be chosen.

There are a lot of reasons that we are able to use the DBSCAN algorithm for our needs. This algorithm is going to be a good one to use to find associations and structures in data that might be hard to get manually, but that is still useful and relevant to help you predict trends and find the patterns that you want. Clustering methods are going to be used in a lot of industries, and you will be able to use the DBSCAN to handle a lot of this as well along the way.

Any time that your business needs to work with an algorithm that can cluster together different points, the DBSCAN algorithm is a good one to use, it is a simple idea that you can reverse and do work in more than one method at the same time, and it can really help you to see which points belong to each cluster in no time as well.

The good news with this one is that this is an algorithm that a lot of programmers already use, which means that you will not need to go through and do the implementation on your own. You are able to use one of the various python packages or libraries in order to handle it. It is also able to work with R, Matlab, and Python. This is a also great way to separate out the data points that you have while making sure that you can get it all set up and ready to go in no time at all. When you are ready to put this to work for your needs, take a look at some of the options of clustering algorithms that are above to help you get started.

Chapter 9: Reduction of Dimensionality

Lastly, let us look at reduction and dimensionality. We are going to spend our time working with both the principal component analysis, and the linear discriminant analysis. We will then compare the two in order to figure out which is the best one to work with, and if we would want to work with each one individually or together. Let's dive in and see what the PCA and LDA are all about.

The Principal Component Analysis

The first option that we need to take a look at here is going to be the Principal Component Analysis or PCA. This is going to be one of those techniques that we are able to use with machine learning that will help us to work with the identification of a smaller number of variables that are uncorrelated, but they are known as the principal components that come from a much larger data set that we are working with.

This technique is going to emphasize on the variation of our data, and then it will capture some of the stronger patterns that are found in the set of data. Simply put, we are going to take some random variables out of our set of data, and then we are going to make sure they are not correlated, outside of being in the same data. But we hope to use these to help us figure out some of the strong patterns and predictions that are found in your set of data as well.

This is an analysis tool that was invented in 1901 by Karl Pearson, and it is going to be used in a number of different types of applications, including exploratory data analysis and predictive models. This analysis is going to be one of the statistical methods, and we will be able to use it in many industries, including computer graphics, neuroscience, face recognition, and image compression to name a few options.

The PCA is going to help us take our data and will make it easier to explore and visualize how this will work and what is inside of that data. It is going to be a pretty simple technique to work with, and it is non-parametric. And when it is used properly, it is going to help us to take out some of the most useful information that we need to form confusing and complex sets of data overall.

This form analysis is also going to focus its attention on the maximum variance amount with the fewest number of principal components as well. This is done to help us learn as much from the data while using as few data points as possible along the way. When we are able only to use a few points of data to get things done, we will find that it is much easier to make some of the predictions that we want, without having to worry about getting confused and lost with a lot of data.

There are a lot of advantages that come with using the PCA, but one of the distinct advantages that come with this is that once the patterns re-found in the data that you are looking for, you will also find support for compressing the data. One will be able to make sure of the PCA to help eliminate the number of variables that you are working with, or when there are going to be too many predictors present in your work compared to how many observations so that you avoid a problem that is known as multicollinearity.

Another thing that you may notice about the PCA is that it is going to be able to relate closely to the canonical correlation analysis, and will even use something known as the orthogonal transformation. The reason that it uses both of these is to help it convert the observations that you are using into a set of values that will then be the principal components.

The number of these principal components that we are going to use in this kind of analysis is going to be either less than or equal to the lesser number of observations that you want to work with as well. The PCA is going to be pretty sensitive when it comes to the relative scaling of the originally used variables.

There are many times when you will want to use this kind of analysis. For example, it is going to be used in any industry that relies on a large set of data, the social sciences, and market research. This technique can also help to provide us with a lower-dimensional picture of some of the data that we originally had. Only a minimal amount of effort is going to be needed when you use this analysis, even when you are trying to reduce all of that data that is confusing and overwhelming into a simplified set of information that you are able to use.

Linear Discriminant Analysis

Now that we know about the PCA, it is time for us to take a look at a Linear Discriminant Analysis or LDA, and how it is going to be used in machine learning in a slightly different manner than the first one that we talked about. In the LDA, we are going to find a well-established technique of machine learning and classification method that is going to be good at predicting the categories that we need the main advantages that we have with this one compared to some of the other classification algorithms is that the model is going to be easy to interpret, and they are good at making predictions as well.

The LDA is going to be used on a regular basis as a dimensionality reduction technique, and this can make it really easy to work with when you want to handle either classification or pattern recognition in some of your programs in machine learning.

The LDA is going to take a set of data cases, which is going to be known as the observations, and will use this as the input. For each of these cases, you will need to make sure that there is a categorical variable because these are responsible for defining the class, and then we need to have at least a few predictor variables, and we are going to see that these are numeric.

Often we are going to be able to take this input data and visualize it as a matrix, with each of the cases being a row, and then each of the variables being in a column. We can think about each of these cases as a point that will show up in the N-dimensional space. N is going to be the number of variables that we are using as predictors. Every point is going to be labeled by its category to make things a little bit easier.

The algorithm that we can use with LDA is going to use this data to help divide up the space of our predictor variables into regions. These regions are a bit more unique, and we are going to label them based on the categories that we can use, and they will have boundaries that are linear, which is where we get the L in our LDA. The model is going to work at predicting the category of a new unseen case, and it can do this according to which region it is going to lie in. The model will be able to predict that all cases that are inside one of these regions that we created are going to belong to the same category. And as long as we trained the algorithm in the proper manner, this is going to hold true.

The linear boundaries are going to happen because we assume that the predictor variables that we are able to get for each category are going to come with the same multivariate Gaussian distribution. This assumption is not always going to be true in practice, it is going to be fairly accurate, and if it is valid like this, then it is possible that the LDA will still be able to perform well and give us the insights and predictions that we need.

In a mathematical manner, this LDA is going to use the input data to help it to derive the necessary coefficients of a scoring function for all of the categories that we need. Each of these functions is able to take as arguments the numeric predictor variables of the case as well. It is then going to scale the variable going to the specific coefficients of that category, as well as the specific output of a score.

The LDA model is going to look at the score that we are going to receive from each function, and then we are able to use the highest score to help us allocate the prediction or the case to a category. We are going to call then the scoring functions, which are important when it comes to helping us make predictions, the discriminant functions.

There are many times when we are able to work with the LDA to help various companies see the results that they would like. To start with, we may find that this can be used with the prediction of bankruptcy. This could happen on accounting ratios and some of the other financial variables. This was actually one of the first methods that were applied to help us explain which firms were able to survive and which ones would enter into bankruptcy.

We can also use the LDA for things like facial recognition. In some of the computerized options for facial recognition, each face is going to be represented with the use of many pixel values. The LDA is able to reduce the number of features that are present in the face to a number that is more manageable before we do the classification. Each of the new dimensions that show up will basically be a combination that is linear to the pixel values, which is then going to form a template. The combinations that are done are going to be known as Fisher's faces, while those that are obtained through the PCA that we talked about before will go by the name of eigenfaces.

Marketing can even work with the LDA on occasion. This can be used to go through a large set of data and distinguish some of the different types of customers and products on the basis of surveys and other forms of data that you were able to collect. These can help us to gather up the data after formulating the problem, estimate the discriminant function, plot the results in the end on a map that we can easily look over and understand in the process as well.

The next place where we are able to work with this is in biomedical studies. This can help us to get an assessment of the severity state of one of your patients and can even give a good prognosis of the outcome of the disease. For example, during the retrospective analysis, patients are going to be divided into groups according to how severe the disease is. Then the results of the analysis, from the clinic and the lab, are going to be studied to help us reveal some of the variables that are different in the studied groups.

When we work with these variables, discriminant functions are going to be built that can help us to classify diseases in the future patient into the severe, moderate, and mild form. This is the same kind of principle that can be used in the biology of different biological groups.

And finally, we will see that the LDA is going to be used to help out with the world of earth sciences in some cases. This method is going to be used to help us to separate out some of the zones of alteration that are there. for example, when we have different data from various zones available to us, this analysis is able to find the pattern within the data and can classify it all in an effective manner.

Comparing PCA and LDA

Now that we have had a chance to talk about the PCA and the LDA options, it is time to take a look at these in comparison to one another. Both of these techniques have a lot to bring to the table and understanding how these are meant to work and how we can combine them to get the best results is going to be imperative to some of the work that we can accomplish with them.

Both the PCA and LDA are going to be techniques of a linear transformation. One option that we are going to see here is that the LDA is going to be a supervised method of machine learning, while the PCA is going to be an example of unsupervised machine learning. This is because the PCA is going to ignore some of the class labels that are there.

A good way to look t the PCA is that it is one of the techniques that you can use that will find the directions of the maximal variance. On the other hand, the LDA is going to work to find a feature subspace in the data that is able to maximize the separability of the class.

Remember, in this that LDA is going to make some assumptions about the classes that are normally distributed and the covariance of the equal classes. This can be important based on some of the algorithms and projects that you are trying to work with along the way.

Many times there is going to be a lot of confusion for programmers when it is time to decide if they should use the LDA or PCA options for their applications. This is often because they are not going to understand some of the fundamental differences that happen between the LDA and PCA. Hopefully, with some of the help of the rest of this section, we are able to get a better idea of how these are similar and how they are separate.

Both the LDA and the PCA are going to be used in the pre-processing step when it comes to problems of pattern recognition and machine learning. The outcome that you are trying to get with both the LDA and PCA is that it will reduce the dimensions that are in our set of data with a minimal amount of information lost in the process. This is going to help reduce the costs of computation along the way, it can speed up how long the computation takes, and can really reduce the issues of overfitting because we are able to project our data over to a lower-dimensional space that will be able to describe the data a bit better.

The main difference that we are going to see between these two is that the PCA is an algorithm that is unsupervised because it is going to ignore the labels of the classes while working to maximize the variance that is able to show up in the set of data. The LDA is going to be slightly different as it is a supervised technique because it is going to compute the directions that are most likely to represent the axes that maximize the separation between the various classes as well.

When we are working with the LDA, rather than just finding the eigenvectors that will maximize the variance of the data, we are also going to have some interest in the axes that are able to maximize how much separation is going to show up between more than one classes. This is important because it is going to help us get this separability to the set of the data, which is something that will be ignored in many cases when it comes to the PCA.

Another difference that we are going to see with this one is that with PCA, we are not going to have the assumptions in place that the points of data are distributed in a normal way. But if the points of data come to us from other distributions, then the PCA is only able to approximate their features through the first few moments. This means that it is not going to be the most optimal options to go with unless the data points are being distributed in a normal manner.

Then we can switch it over to looking at the LDA. IN this situation, you are going to assume that the points of data that we are looking at are going to come to us from two separate multivariate normal distributions that have different means, while still having a covariance matrix that is the same. What this does for us is give us a more generalized method out of the LDA compared to what we are able to see with the PCA.

It is also important to figure out when and how we would visualize the plots that are needed with both LDA and PCA. The plots have been generated for these two algorithms with the help of the Scikit-Learn machine learning library, and with the help of the Iris Dataset. This is a good one to work with because it has 150 images of flowers in three classes, and each flower is going to come with 4 features. You would then be able to work with both of the options above in order to help you to figure out which flower, off of some images that you have, fit into each category.

This is going to bring up the question of when you would want to work with the PCA method and when you would want to work with the LDA method. As we have been going through this part of the guidebook, it may seem like the LDA is going to be the best technique to go with most of the time, but usually, this is not going to be the case. Comparisons will show us over time that the PCA method is often going to be able to outperform the LDA, if the number of samples that are in a class is relatively small, such as what we would be able to find in that Iris data set from above.

However, if you are planning on working with a really big set of data that has a lot of classes, the PCA is not going to work as well with this one, and it is important to work with the LDA method instead. This is due to the fact that class separability is going to be an important factor in helping us make sure that we are also reducing the dimensionality.

One final note before we finish off with this idea is that it is possible to work with the PCA and the LDA together. This will allow you to get some of the benefits of both of these options, without having to worry about some of the negatives with them as much. There are many opportunities when we need to use this kind of option, but it can really add to another level of power when it is time to handle some of the data that we have with machine learning.

Conclusion

Thank you for making it through to the end of *Python Machine Learning*, let's hope it was informative and able to provide you with all of the tools you need to achieve your goals whatever they may be.

The next step is to start working with some of the different algorithms that we have in this guidebook. There are many times when working with machine learning and good data analysis will be able to help your company to see some results. But first, you need to take the time to collect the right data and then run it through a properly trained and tested algorithm to help you get the right insights and predictions that you need.

These are just some of the topics that we are going to explore when it comes to machine learning, and one of those is being able to pick out the right algorithm for machine learning, and figuring out how to put data through each one to make it work is going to be hard. There are just so many Python machine learning algorithms out there, and many of them sound great that it can be confusing to know how to make them run the way that you want.

This is why this guidebook spent time exploring the different algorithms, and discussed in-depth information about how these work and what you are able to do with each one. The most of common algorithms like neural networks, random forests and decision trees, clustering, KNN, have been discussed as well. When you are done, you will have a good idea of how to work with machine learning and how to make all of this work on your machine learning project.

There are many times when you may decide to work with data analysis or some of the other parts of machine learning, and knowing which algorithms to choose is going to be imperative to this process.

If you found this book useful in any way, a review on Amazon is always appreciated !

Josh Hugh Learning